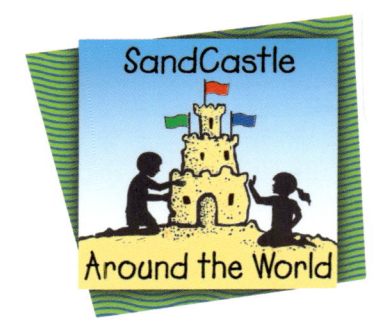

People
Around the World

Kelly Doudna

Consulting Editor, Diane Craig, M.A./Reading Specialist

Published by ABDO Publishing Company, 4940 Viking Drive, Edina, Minnesota 55435.

Copyright © 2004 by Abdo Consulting Group, Inc. International copyrights reserved in all countries. No part of this book may be reproduced in any form without written permission from the publisher. SandCastle™ is a trademark and logo of ABDO Publishing Company.

Printed in the United States.

Credits
Edited by: Pam Price
Curriculum Coordinator: Nancy Tuminelly
Cover and Interior Design and Production: Mighty Media
Photo Credits: BananaStock Ltd., Comstock, Corbis Images, Creatas, Digital Vision

Library of Congress Cataloging-in-Publication Data

Doudna, Kelly, 1963-
    People around the world / Kelly Doudna.
      p. cm. -- (Around the world)
    Includes index.
    Summary: Describes the many groups of people found around the world.
    ISBN 1-59197-567-0
     1. Ethnology--Juvenile literature. 2. Indigenous peoples--Juvenile literature. [1. Ethnology. 2. Culture.] I. Title.

GN333.D68 2004
305.8--dc22

2003062950

SandCastle™ books are created by a professional team of educators, reading specialists, and content developers around five essential components that include phonemic awareness, phonics, vocabulary, text comprehension, and fluency. All books are written, reviewed, and leveled for guided reading, early intervention reading, and Accelerated Reader® programs and designed for use in shared, guided, and independent reading and writing activities to support a balanced approach to literacy instruction.

Let Us Know

After reading the book, SandCastle would like you to tell us your stories about reading. What is your favorite page? Was there something hard that you needed help with? Share the ups and downs of learning to read. We want to hear from you! To get posted on the ABDO Publishing Company Web site, send us e-mail at:

sandcastle@abdopub.com

SandCastle Level: Fluent

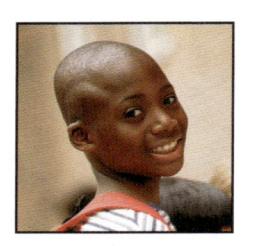

People around the world look different from each other.

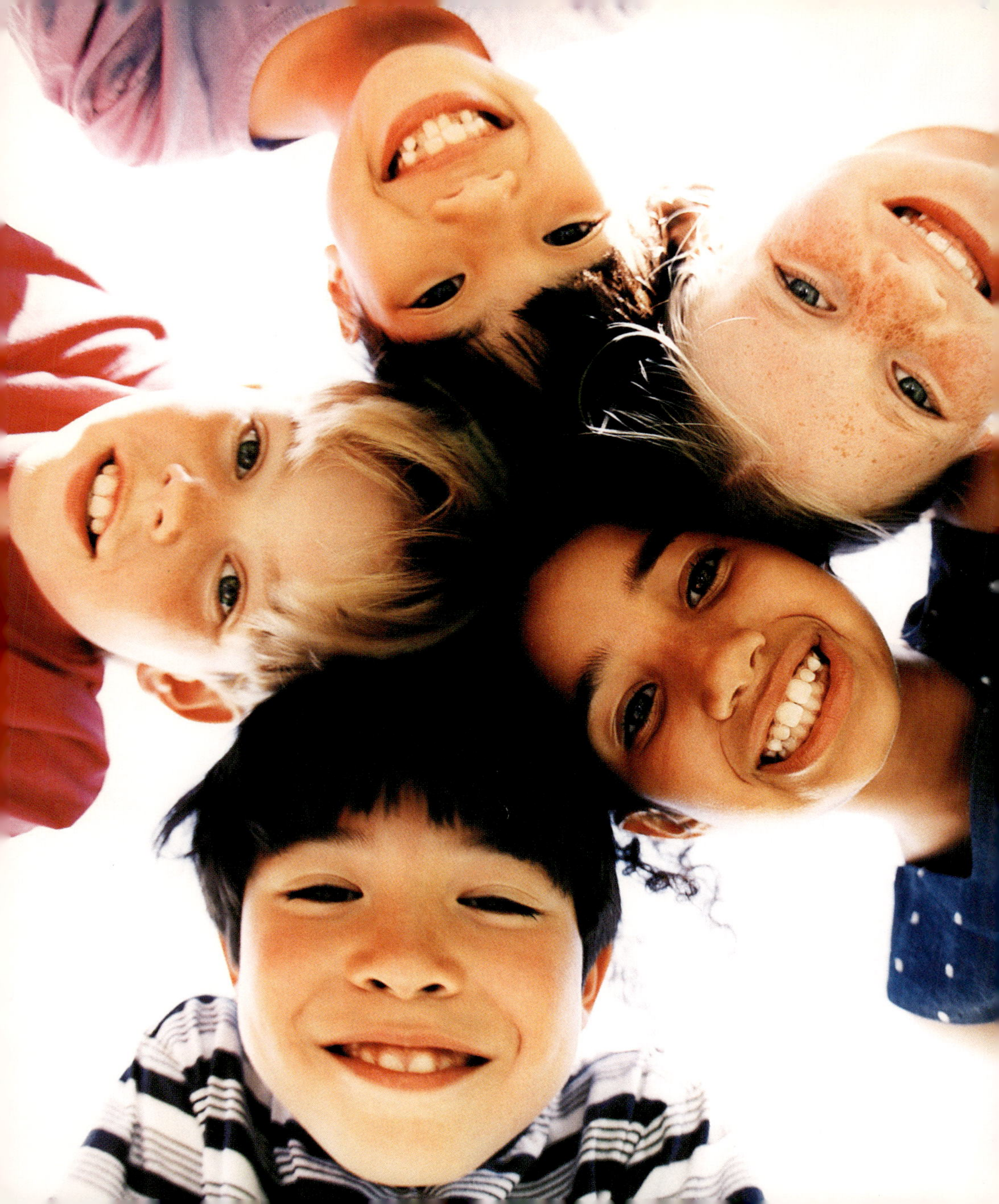

Understanding and accepting these differences is important.

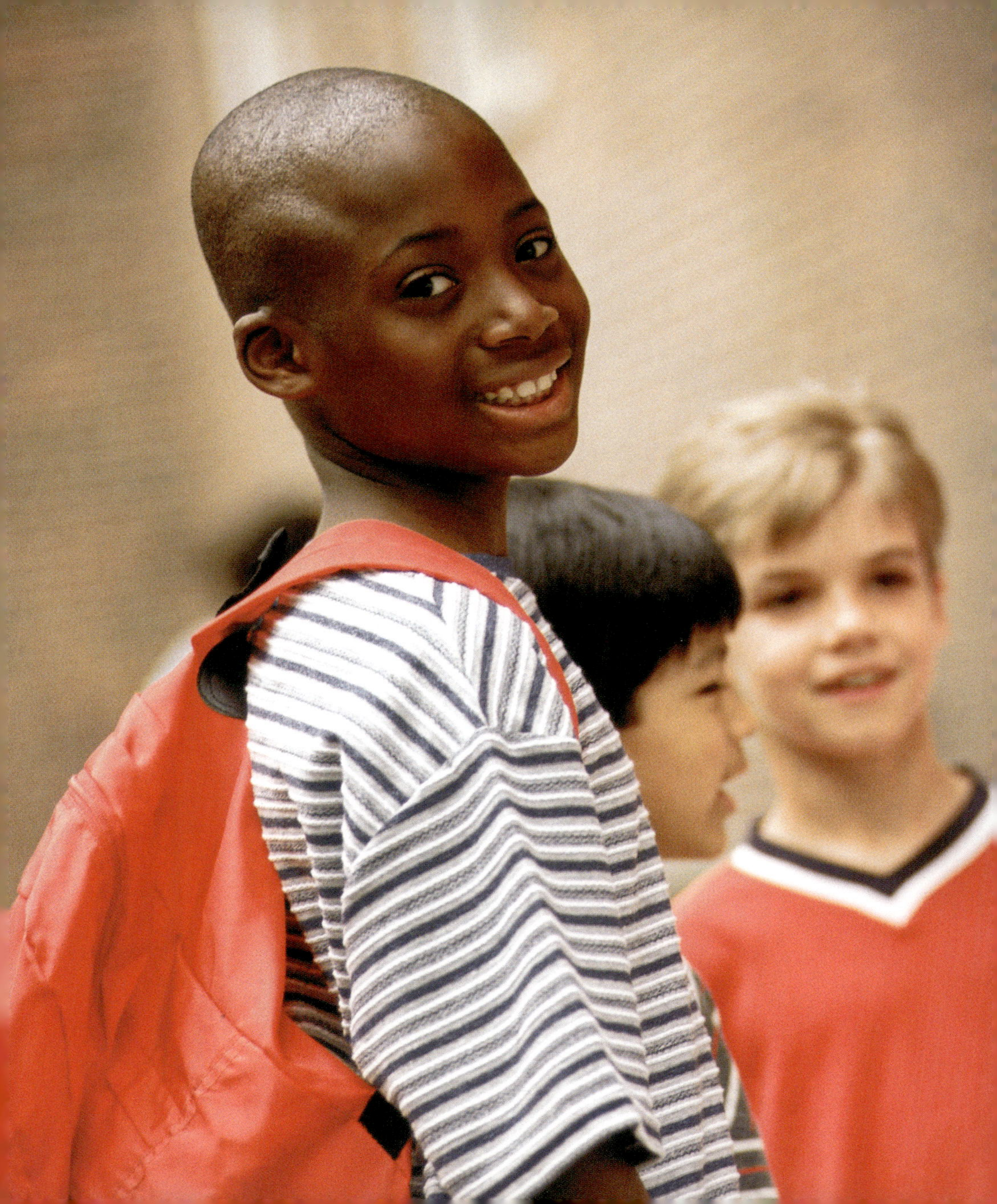

It makes the world a more peaceful place to live.

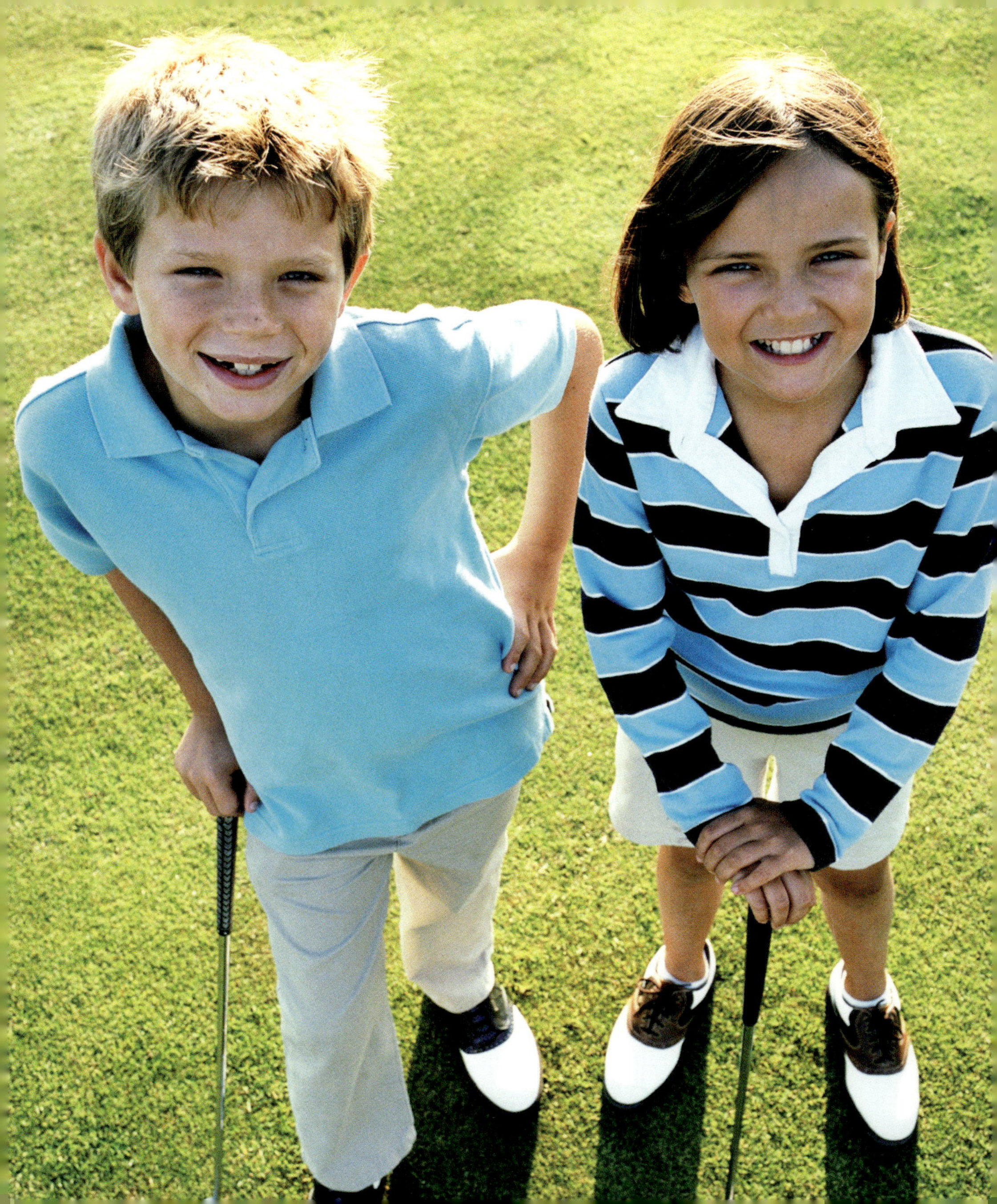

Don and Claire are white.

They live in Scotland.

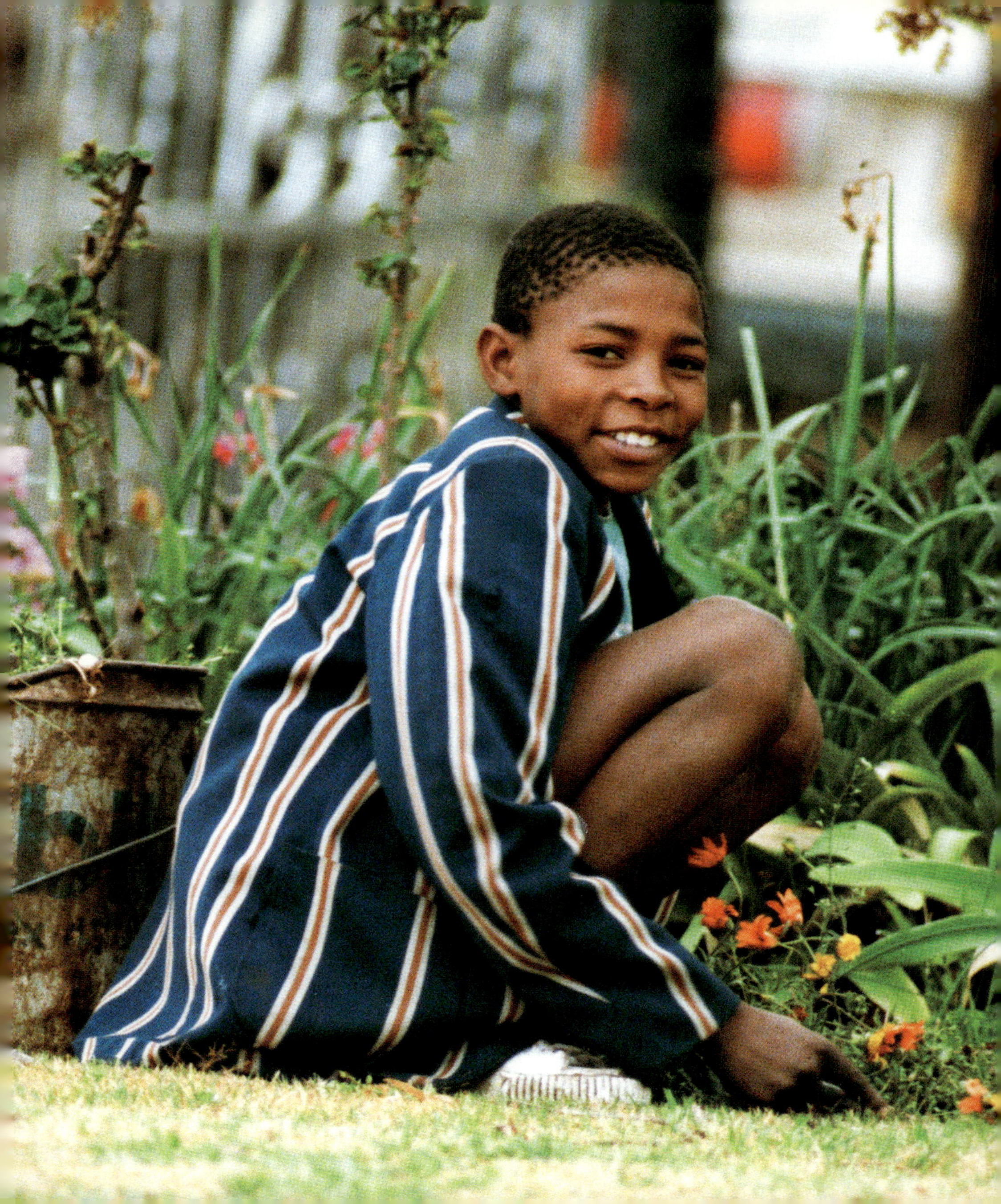

Ulan is black.

He lives in South Africa.

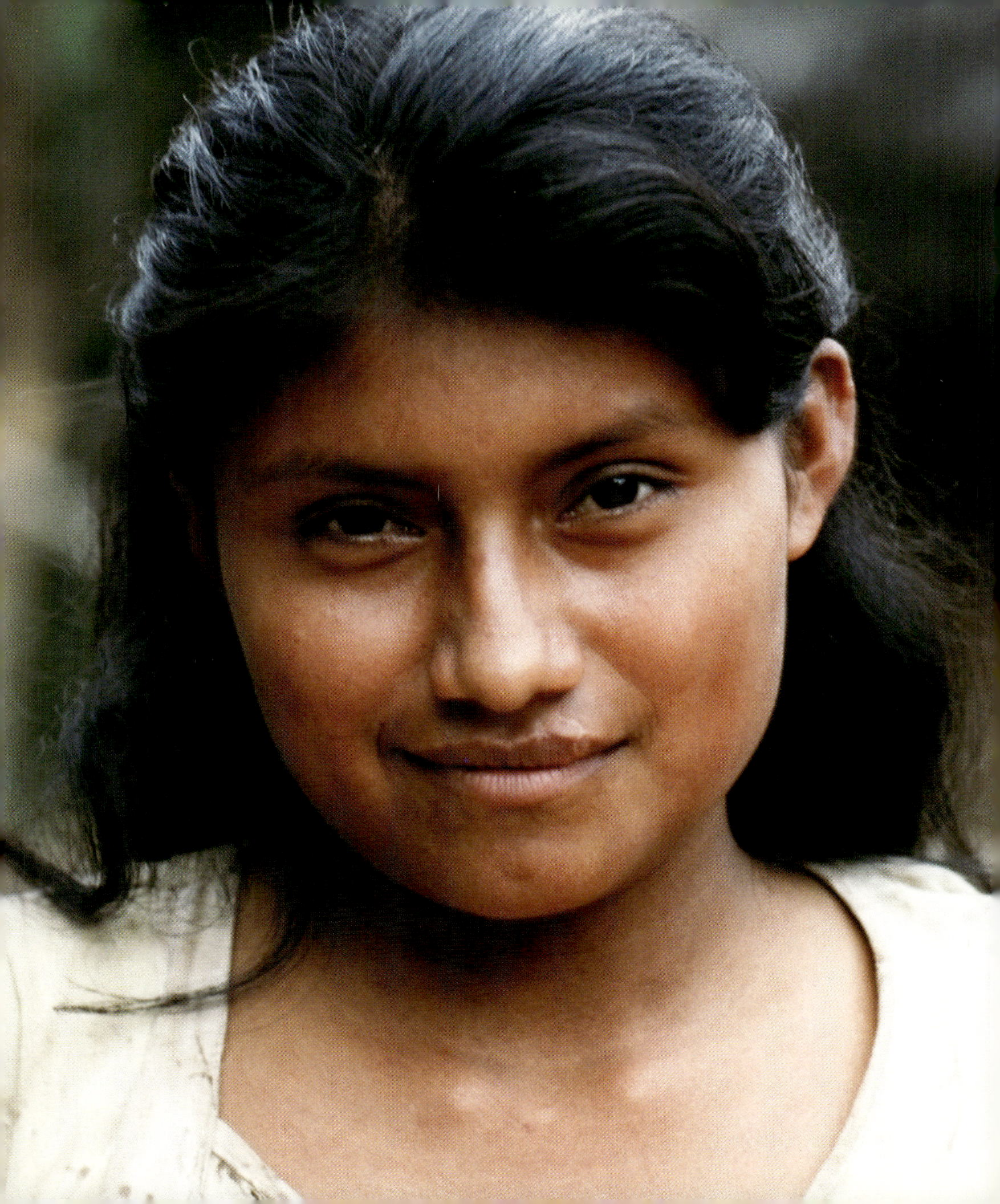

Ana is Latina.

She lives in Guatemala.

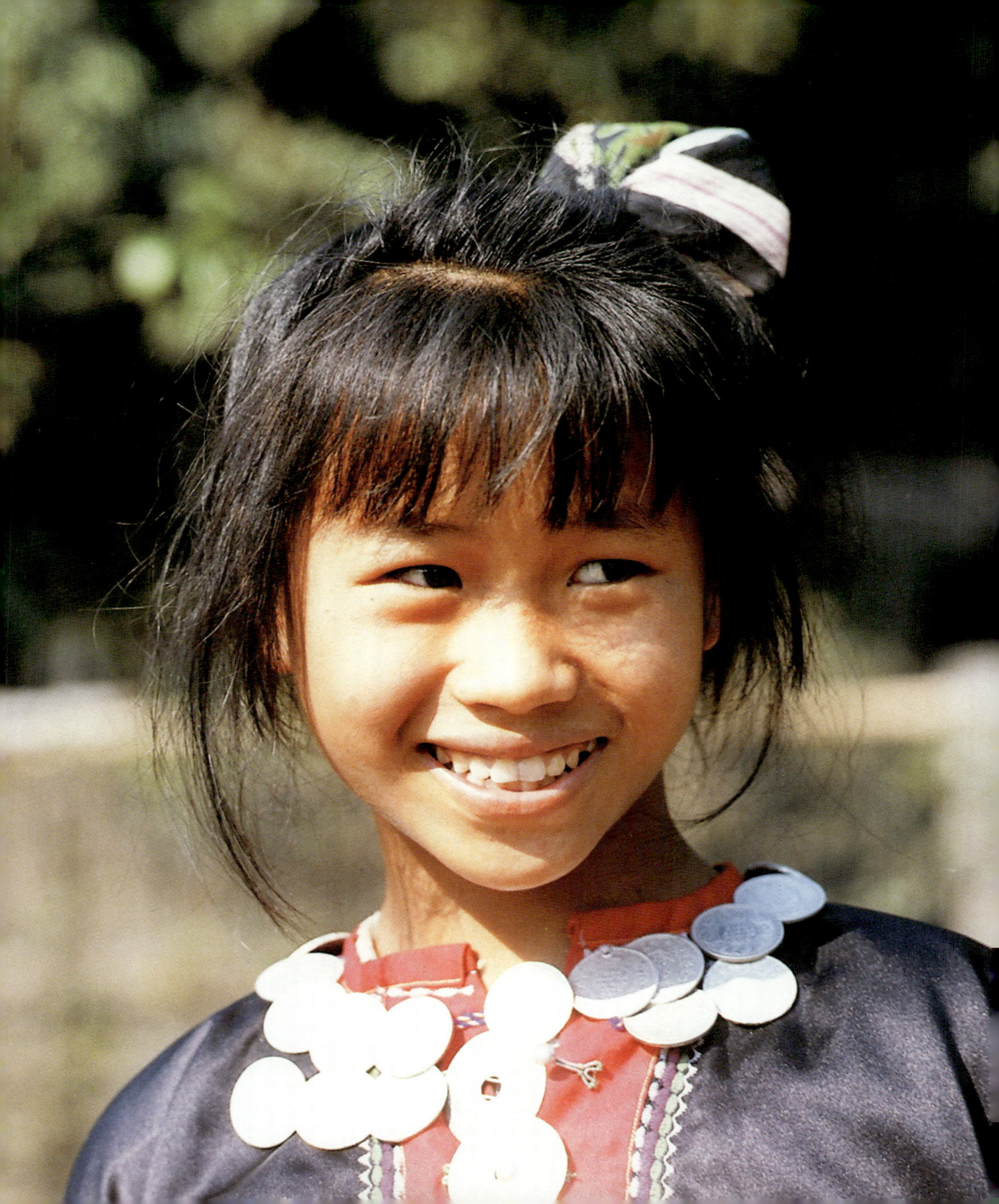

Mali is Asian.

She lives in Thailand.

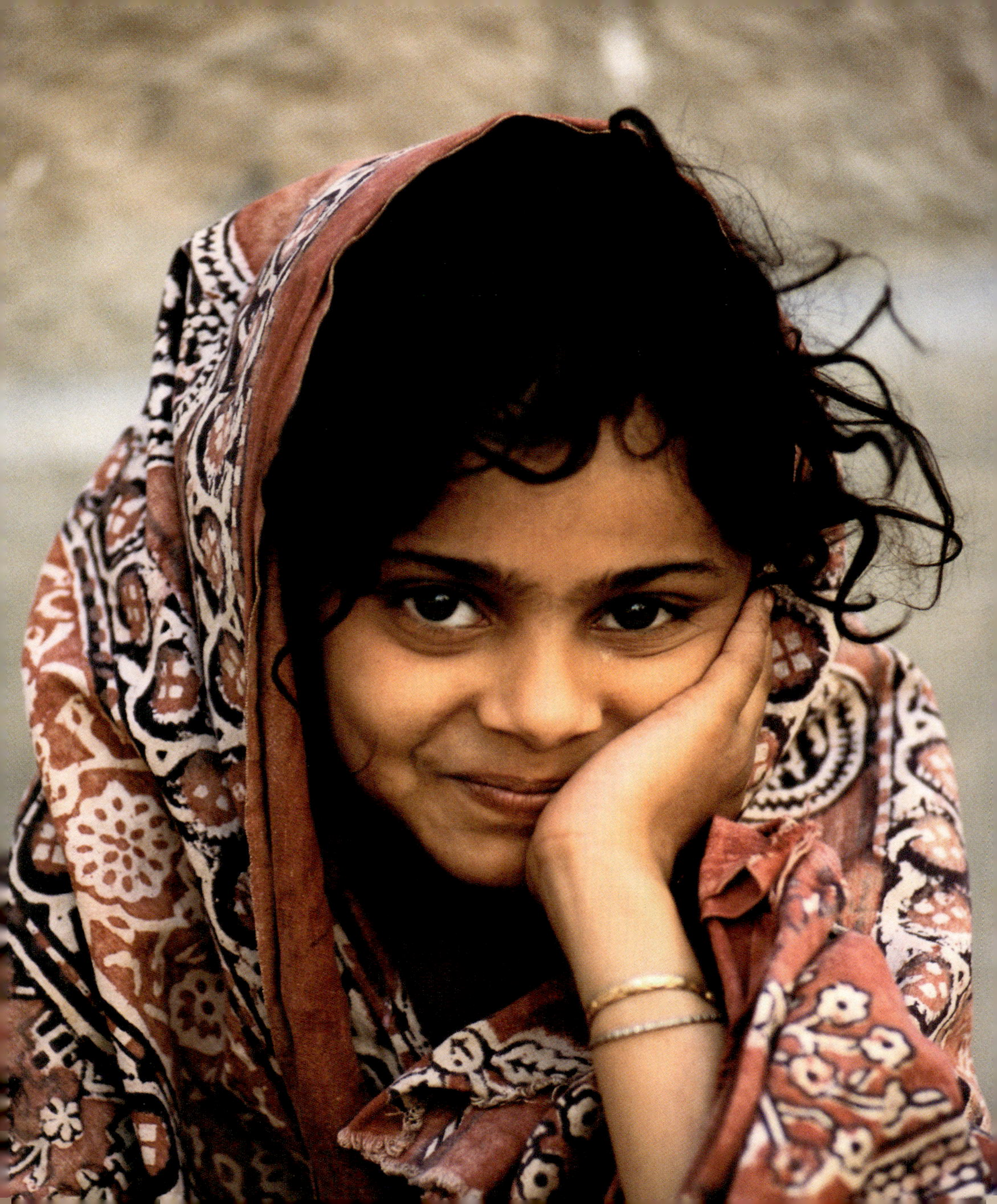

Zita is Arabic.

She lives in Kuwait.

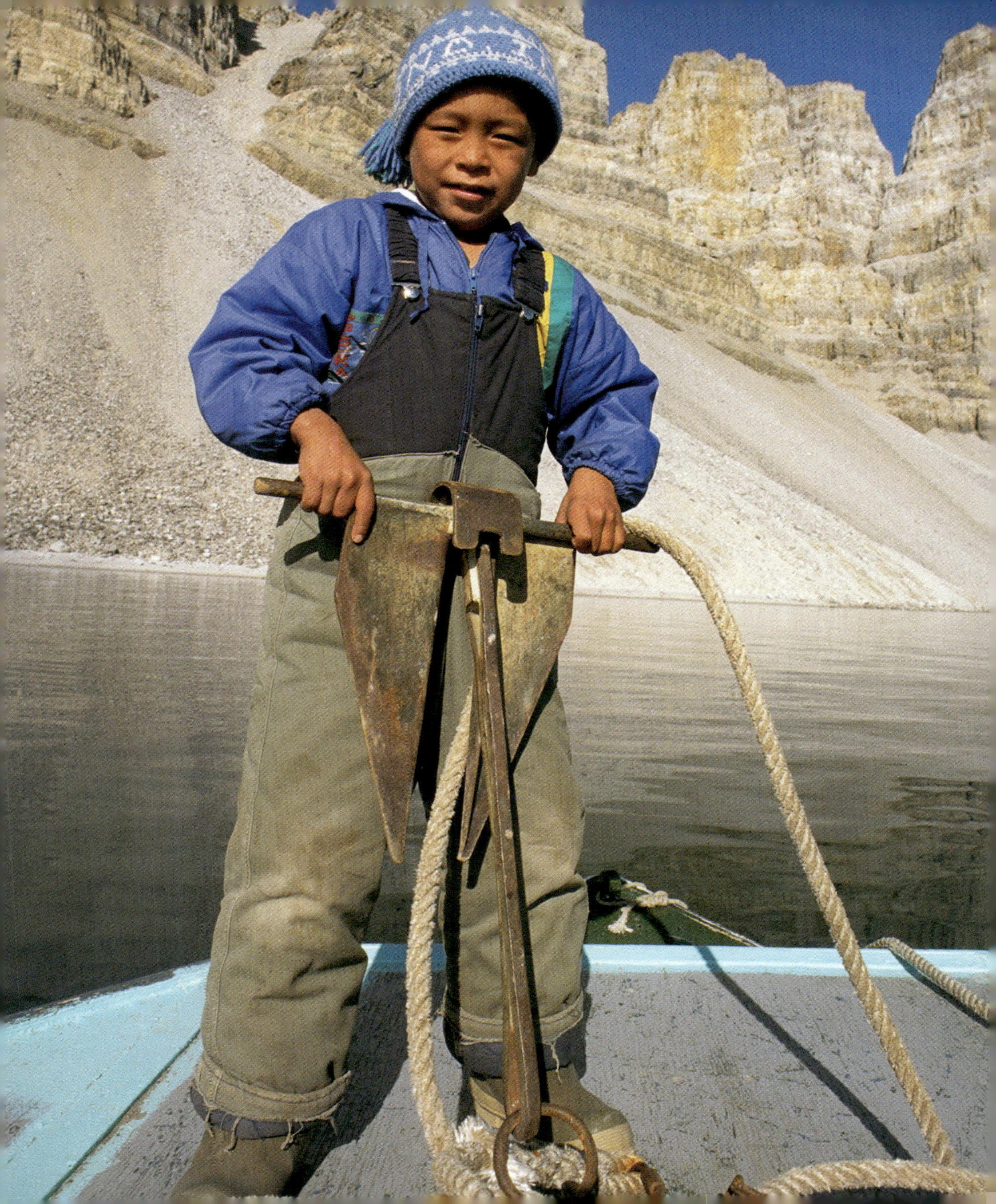

Yana is Inuit.

He lives in Canada.

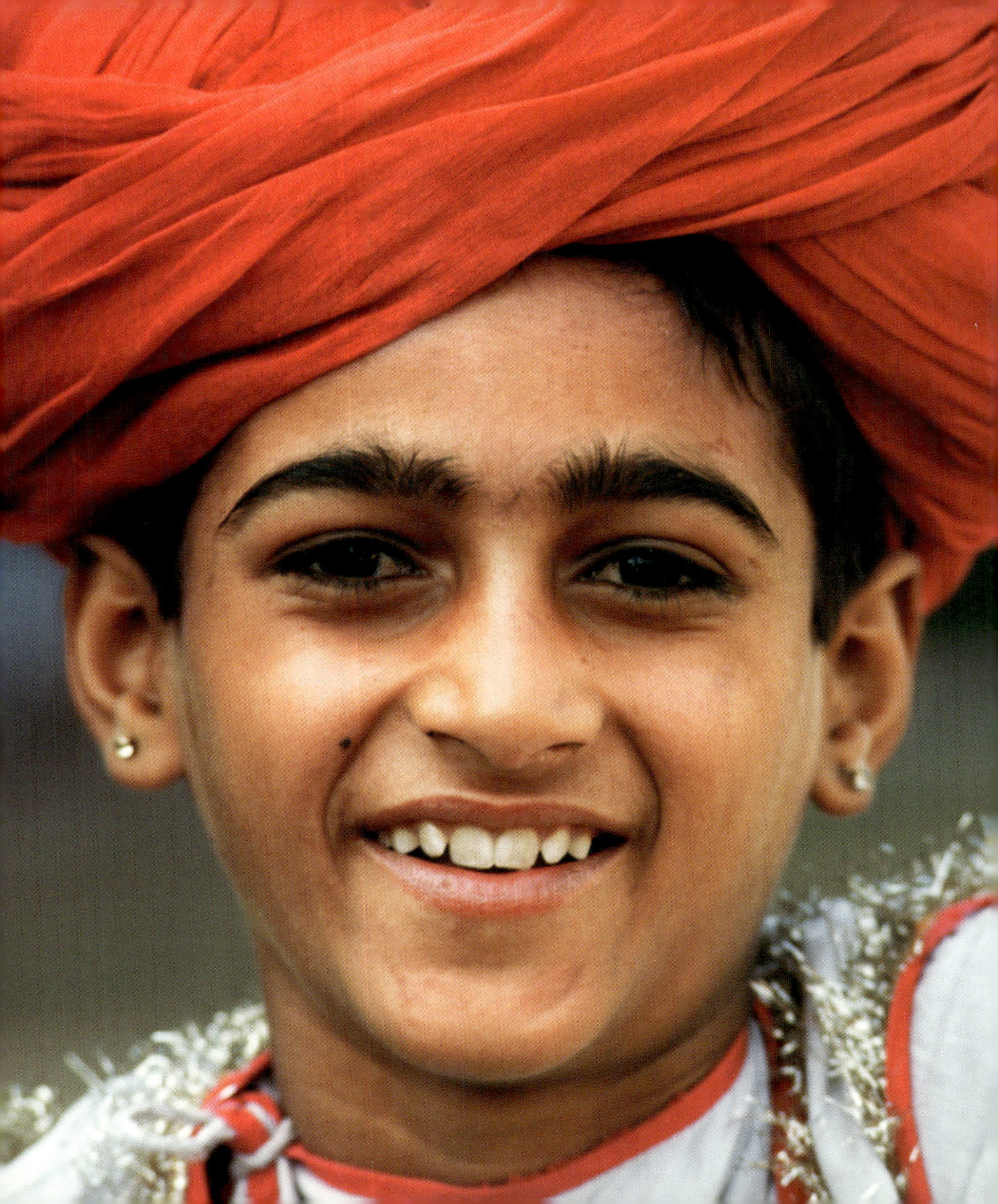

Do you know people who look different than you?

Did You Know?

Nunavut is the newest Canadian province. It was created in 1999 by dividing the Northwest Territories. Its population is 85 percent Inuit.

Over one billion people live in China. That's more than in any other country.

Golfer Tiger Woods describes himself as "Cablinasian," a mixture of Caucasian, black, American Indian, and Asian.

Kenya is a diverse country. It has 42 tribes or tribal groupings.

Glossary

accept. to think of as normal, right, or unavoidable

different. not alike

important. of significant value or impact

peaceful. calm, free from disagreement

place. a particular space or location

understand. to know well due to close contact or experience

world. the planet Earth

About SandCastle™

A professional team of educators, reading specialists, and content developers created the SandCastle™ series to support young readers as they develop reading skills and strategies and increase their general knowledge. The SandCastle™ series has four levels that correspond to early literacy development in young children. The levels are provided to help teachers and parents select the appropriate books for young readers.

Emerging Readers
(no flags)

Beginning Readers
(1 flag)

Transitional Readers
(2 flags)

Fluent Readers
(3 flags)

These levels are meant only as a guide. All levels are subject to change.

ABDO Publishing Company

To see a complete list of SandCastle™ books and other nonfiction titles from ABDO Publishing Company, visit www.abdopub.com or contact us at:

4940 Viking Drive, Edina, Minnesota 55435 • 1-800-800-1312 • fax: 1-952-831-1632